HOW I BECAME A
Psychic Artist

HOW I BECAME A
Psychic
Artist

DORIS STRODE

ATHENA PRESS
LONDON

How I Became a Psychic Artist
Copyright ©Doris Strode 2007

All Rights Reserved

No part of this book may be reproduced in any form
by photocopying or by any electronic or mechanical means,
including information storage or retrieval systems,
without permission in writing from both the copyright
owner and the publisher of this book.

ISBN (10 digit) 1 84401 889 X
ISBN (13 digit) 978 1 84401 889 5

First Published 2007 by
ATHENA PRESS
Queen's House, 2 Holly Road
Twickenham TW1 4EG
United Kingdom

Printed for Athena Press

Contents

My Early Life	7
The Circle	17
A Selection of Spiritual Guides	29
The Venerable Bede	30
Doctor Adams	32
Sister Anne (A Nun)	34
Su Shan Long	36
Wai Lai (Chinaman from the Ming Dynsasty)	38
Elizabeth Barrett Browning	40
Sister Isobel Bayliss	42
Megan (Romany Gypsy)	44
Doctor Adams	46
Doctor Basehart	48
Tia-le-Sonn	50
Rising Moon	52

Pocahontas 54

Red Wing (Cherokee) 56

Red Wing Camp 58

Before the Circle

*M*ANY years ago, when I was very young, I became quite interested in certain things my mother would tell me; indeed, these things fascinated me. She told me that she could see spirits. It was amazing that she had the ability to see these spirits so plainly. You see, she was a natural clairvoyant.

Clairvoyants do not always see in the same manner; for instance, I see clearly with my eyes shut. It is similar to looking at a coloured photograph or a television but, unlike my mother who was a natural-born medium, I had to work for several years in a development circle before I could reach the same level of ability.

I would like to give you an insight into my life right from the beginning so that you can understand the determination and patience I had to acquire in order to overcome all obstacles. If you are determined, anything is possible.

I will begin by explaining my mother's life when she was young and single. She was rather a timid woman and lived with her father (her mother sadly died when she was fourteen). Unfortunately, although very gifted, she was unable to use her skills professionally. I can remember my mother being very neat and tidy, always with pearls around her neck, and her hair neatly done.

The story that I am about to tell you now, regarding events that happened to my mother, has always fascinated me.

She was very close to her cousin Lily, who used to pop in nearly every day after work for a cup of tea and gossip. When her cousin Lily didn't arrive for four or five days in a row, my mother became rather worried and puzzled as it was very unusual for her to stay away for so long. She felt increasingly uneasy; then there was a knock on the door and there stood Lily.

My mother said, 'Hello Lily, I wondered what had happened to you! Come in and I'll put the kettle on for some tea.' Thinking that Lily had followed her in, she turned around and, to her surprise, Lily had vanished! Then my mother realised that Lily had come to say goodbye. A short while later, my mother's father, John, came in from work looking rather grave.

'I am afraid I have bad news for you, my dear.'

'I know,' said my mother. 'Lily's dead.'

John was astonished and exclaimed, 'How did you know?'
My mother did not answer.

Later, my mother met my father and they were married. My father was a very immaculate man and a perfectionist, which I found rather hard to live up to.

Although he was very strict with my two older brothers and me, I had to admire him: he had high standards and second best simply would not do. I can remember my mother looking out of the window to see if he was coming home from business so that she could put the kettle on for tea. He was chief clerk at the Stock Exchange in Threadneedle Street in London. It was his one and only job and he worked there until he retired. In those days one retired with a hundred pounds and a gold watch. It doesn't sound much now, but back then it was a lot of money.

After he retired, he mellowed quite a bit. I suppose in his day it was quite a responsibility to look after a family, especially with his high standards. My mother wanted to go to work during the war but he would not hear of it. He said it would be a 'slight on his character'. He was quite Victorian in his ways and was a very proud man.

Things were very different in those days. We didn't have social services or allowances of any kind. If you didn't work, you didn't eat. If you didn't pay the rent or mortgage you were either on the street or in the workhouse. It was so much harder then. Fortunately, he kept us in quite a comfortable way; we did not want for anything. This is why I admired him. He had high principles and a sense of duty. We lived in a nice semi-detached house in Surbiton; quite a respectable location with tree-lined avenues and grass lawns.

I think what really fascinated me were the tales my mother used to tell me of the many things that had happened to her in her life. The story of Cousin Lily was just one of them. I have been extremely interested in Spiritualism ever since.

Once, all agog, I asked my mother, 'What do spirits look like?'

'Exactly the same as us,' she said, 'except they have a radiance about them.'

Before the Circle

I remember that when my son was twelve years old, my mother told me that she could see several spirit forms in one of our bedrooms. She asked me not to mention this to my son as it would make him a little nervous.

What a pity she could not use her gift to help and comfort people, but my father did not understand. Indeed, she did not tell him anything about it, knowing full well she would never have been believed or he would have thought her very odd. Times were different then. She also had a family to look after. I think she confided in me because she had to tell someone. We used to go for Sunday walks in the country and sometimes she would sing little French songs – she was half French by her father and was brought up by a French aunt after her mother died. My mother could remember when she was very young and lived in Bethnal Green. It was a rural place then. She remembered the weaving looms upstairs in their cottage; her parents and ancestors came over to England as silk weavers, originally with the Huguenots.

My mother was quite a good pianist but my father was rather critical so she only played when he went out. We were all made to play the piano and detested this because he was such a hard taskmaster and while we were made to play for an hour each day, other children were outside having fun. I was sent to a music school once a week but was nervous of playing in front of my father since, being of a rather fiery nature, he could easily lose his temper. After the war, my father himself joined three orchestras in which he played the flute. Every Sunday morning we listened to scales and music which, I may say, wasn't really appreciated but we didn't dare say anything!

As a child I was rather shy. I remember my grandfather saying, 'She lives in a world of her own.' I was quite pretty then, although I didn't realise it as I wasn't very confident. I remember that when I was quite little, a neighbour said I looked like a piece of Dresden china. This puzzled me quite a bit because I hadn't the faintest idea what Dresden china was. It is funny how things stick in one's mind.

At of the age fourteen I went to an art college for four years. I was very happy there. We had a wonderful time, although we had a lot of homework. The first year of art college we covered quite a

How I Became a Psychic Artist

variety of topics: painting flowers and plants; memory drawing (for instance, depicting a church inside and out once you had seen it); perspective; plans and elevations; geometry; architecture; and finally life drawing – which I was quite good at although I had difficulty with people's faces. It seems strange because now I draw them very easily with the help of the spirits.

After the first year we decided which subject we wanted to pursue. I wanted to work in an advertising agency at that time. I was at the art college for four years, by which time the Second World War had unfortunately started and I had to think very carefully about my future. We were not allowed luxury trades so that ruled out art. I was very disappointed, of course, and rather fed up. I either had to enlist in the ATS or Land Army, or be a civil servant employed in a government job. I was fortunate enough to be offered a post as the latter, working for the Army Pay Corps at Finsbury Circus, London. I collated mail and wrote to the soldiers who were absent without leave and also did several other administrative jobs. I was eighteen at the time.

To get to work every day, I left home at 5 a.m. to arrive by 8 a.m. which meant I had to travel in the dark. I went from Berrylands, Surbiton to Waterloo on the train and then on the underground to Finsbury Park, treading over people that were still asleep. You may find this strange but quite a few Londoners slept on the underground platforms all night to escape the bombs. You can imagine the devastation above ground: there was destruction and chaos everywhere. There were often ropes up to stop us going along one or two streets where unexploded bombs had fallen. I was usually in a hurry to get to work but, as there were so many streets cordoned off, I had to keep changing course which made me hopelessly lost and confused.

The dark didn't help either. One week on my way to work at 5 a.m. I had climbed through the cordons in front of the fields that led to Berrylands station each day so that I could cut across and save time. I did not realise how stupid I had been until I returned at the weekend, in daylight, and saw the notice 'UNEXPLODED BOMB: KEEP OUT'. It was quite a shock to think that I had been passing close by all week! From then on I made sure to stick to the path to be safe, even if it was a much longer walk.

Before the Circle

During this time, I met a soldier. He was a corporal and worked in the same building as me and eventually we married. I was twenty-one years old at this time and by the following year I was expecting a baby. However, I still had to work for seven months to get full pay and, believe me, it was no joke, particularly when we had to abandon the trains and walk along the railway lines. I hadn't realised it was such a long way down – very different when you get on the train from a platform – but we took it in our stride as we only did this if there was a raid on and enemy aircraft were above us: it was for our own safety.

Finally I left this job owing to the birth of my son, Michael. I didn't work again for some time as the raids became almost continuous. I remember one day I was walking along the Kingston bypass at Tolworth with my son in a pram, when the sirens went off, warning of an air raid. It was very sudden and I could hear the drone of enemy aircraft overhead and our big guns were firing, which was quite frightening. I was unable to cross the bypass to the shelter of the shops because there were railings all along the road. I had to race all the way to where there was a gap before I could cross over. The shopkeeper was waving and beckoning me to hurry and eventually I reached him, but I could not get the harness off my baby to remove him from the pram. I was all fingers and thumbs! At last I managed to remove the harness and ran through the shop to a brick shed where we took shelter. There we would be safe from the shrapnel and watch the aerial dogfights.

When, at last, the raid was over we emerged from the shed. We had to be careful as there was a lot of broken glass about – the front windows of the shops had been shattered completely. I looked for my pram that had been left outside, but it was nowhere to be seen! Then I spotted it, a long way in the distance and far along the bypass. The force of the blast had sent it flying. All I could see was the shade hanging off – it was a wreck. I couldn't mind about this; I was just thankful we were safe.

After the war I had several jobs. I worked for a Japanese firm in London, painting lampshades to be sold in West End shops such as Selfridges and Harrods. I also worked as a ledger clerk for Freeman's (the catalogue people) in Balham. I eventually left however, because I was moving from South London to Clacton-on-Sea with my husband and children. We stayed in Clacton for about five years until my husband wanted to move to Basingstoke to work.

The next job I had was at a shop called Bellman's, a Scottish firm selling ladies' wear, haberdashery and wools, etc. I was offered a job as senior sales lady for a time, until the manageress left and I was asked to take her place. We were all very happy there and I managed to boost the takings quite considerably. Bellman's had branches all over England and were quite a big concern; they later changed their name to Country Casuals.

My father had been in the First World War – as a sergeant major and a fitness instructor – so naturally he was always very agile. I remember him much later doing his exercises at 6 a.m. every morning. We used to laugh, but the laughs were on us for he certainly benefited by exercising in this way – he had never been ill and never had a cold in his life. If he had an inkling of one he would take whisky at night and it was gone in the morning. In his later years, when in his eighties, he would play bowls and was treasurer of the club at Clacton-on-Sea, for that was where my parents retired.

Unfortunately, he overdid things, walking quite a few miles to the bowling green four times a day and in the heat. Eventually it just caught up with him. He had a headache (the first) and suffered a cerebral haemorrhage. It should have killed him instantly but, being so healthy, he was in a coma for three days. I was hoping in a way that he would die. I know this sounds awful but, had he lived, he would have been like a cabbage with no feeling whatsoever. Imagine the frustration living that way, especially after being so fit. It was kinder to let him die. Naturally we were very upset but we know he is happy now.

How wonderful knowledge of the afterlife is! No death, only a different dimension – a wonderful dimension. As God says, 'In my house there are many mansions', meaning levels. 'Like attracts like'. In other words, you go to wherever is suitable according to

Before the Circle

how you have lived your life, for this is a learning planet. Most of us go to the third plane, some to the fourth. But it is a beautiful and wonderful place full of such peace and happiness. If only people knew, they would not be so sad and heartbroken.

My mother passed over two years before my father. She had been ill with cancer of the pancreas but survived the operation and was at home. One day, the milkman rang the doorbell and, being flustered as she rushed to the front door, she tripped over the blanket which was covering her and landed back in hospital with a broken leg. From then on she got weaker and weaker; it was the shock, I expect. My brother, who was a male nurse at the time, looked after her brilliantly at home. He was very dedicated but she slipped away a year later. I was extremely upset, although I had some knowledge of the spirit world. I wish I had been more enlightened then – it would have been so comforting – but it was not until later, on attending a circle, that I acquired the full knowledge.

At the time of her death I had a shop at Leigh-on-Sea. It sold ladies' wear which was rather slow and it was not making much money. Then, one day, a lady mentioned to me that she was going to the hairdresser's and what a nuisance it was to have to get a bus. I suddenly thought I could also open a hairdressing shop. So, after getting permission from my landlord, I started my new venture. It was a double-fronted shop, so I could use one side for ladies' wear and the other for hair products. I had already modernised the clothing department of the shop but now I had to renovate the back room to be used as a hairdressing salon. My son did a good job of decorating it and I had to order all the hairdryers and dressing-out tables, the curlers, perms, colours and hand basins. It was quite a lot to do but it did look very attractive and professional in pink and black.

All I needed then was to employ a good hairdresser and, after a time, I did manage to employ a really first-class girl called Shirley. Her father was a West End wigmaker in Mayfair. I used to do the shampooing, sweep the floor and hand up the rollers. It may sound odd since I was the owner but Shirley was the hairdresser, so I told her to take charge and I was in charge of the ladies' wear. We worked very well together and had a lot of laughs. She was also interested in

Spiritualism so we had interesting chats together.

Once a month a florist's van came round and I would order a bouquet. One month I would put pastel colours in the window, another autumn colours. I was lucky to be so artistic. It made a big difference to the shop. We were very busy right from the start. Shirley gave me a crash course in hairdressing so that I didn't have to close the salon while she went on holiday. I explained to the customers and they were very understanding.

After five years I was ready for a change, though. I was getting a little fed up with never going out anywhere. Sunday, my one day off, was spent getting prepared for Monday. I also had the ladies' and children's wear, which had picked up quite a bit – but it was like having two businesses under one roof. I also had two daughters who came in at lunchtime, so I also cooked dinner for them!

While I was running the shop, I heard of a woman who had a development circle in Benfleet which I sometimes attended in the evenings until we sold up and moved to Basingstoke.

The Circle

*W*E moved back to Chingford and it was there that I saw an advertisement for a development circle at Leytonstone in the *Psychic News*. I was quite excited about this and first met George and Martha who ran the circle. They lived in a ground-floor maisonette which was very pretty, with loads of flowers and plants. Although they didn't have much garden, George had made it look very attractive. Both he and Martha were very friendly and I felt so much at ease. I felt very comfortable and over the years we became firm friends.

A development circle is a circle where one meditates and learns about spirits and also gets protection from any unwanted spirits. That is how we began. It is most important to meditate, as in meditation you reach a higher level of consciousness and eventually feel a spirit, almost like a feather, touch one's face. After a time this will become much stronger. It is very important to be patient and, of course, completely relaxed.

Naturally, I was quite excited about joining this development circle and found the sitters very friendly. A sitter is a person who wishes to develop by acquiring knowledge and understanding of the spirit world. I was introduced to Phyllis who was the mistress of ceremonies. She always opened the circle with a prayer of address, which was very good. We had Sid who was a healer who rented the Conservative Party meeting rooms and worked there. Then there were Heather and Joan who were very devout and became quite gifted. They had much knowledge and understanding. We also had Robert who had a sense of humour and made us laugh. He was very witty but of course knew his place. Derek and Gerald were also very keen sitters.

The important thing was we all got on together and there was perfect harmony. This is essential in a circle as the spirit guides cannot work with you otherwise. George used to talk in a trance, giving us lots of wonderful information regarding spirits, and we all got to know our guides who talked to us through him. After a time, I found my throat was getting very sore after meditation. I questioned this but the spirits said they were trying to build a voice box. Strange, really, because I wanted to develop into a psychic artist, but they sometimes have plans that we don't know about. I was rather intrigued by this and my throat felt stiff, like

How I Became a Psychic Artist

wood. This lasted for a few months. Then, one day, Red Wing, one of my guides, suddenly spoke through me, and boomed out his name in a deep, strong voice which was quite the opposite of mine. We were all in meditation at that point and had to laugh afterwards because it had made everyone jump like anything.

As the weeks went on, I had a few more words from Red Wing until I was having quite a conversation. It was fascinating when my fellow sitters all told me what had been said. At the time I was aware of some things – it was as though someone else was talking – but as soon as I had finished a sentence, I couldn't remember any of it. It was erased. This seemed quite weird at first, but I soon got used to it and after about a year, I acquired another guide, a Doctor Andrews, who spoke completely differently. And then, after a time, I also acquired a Chinaman called Wai Lai. He was so fascinating and very Chinese in his mannerisms; the Doctor was extremely cultured and used very long words. In the meantime in meditation I began to see figures and eventually I saw the other circle members' guides. One by one, I painted all the guides for them.

Wai Lai, the Chinese guide, informed us of his way of life while on the earth plane. He belonged to the Ming dynasty and worked for the emperor as a scribe. He was very wise and knew when to keep quiet and had much tact and decorum as, he said, he didn't wish to lose his head. We laughed at this: he could be quite funny at times.

I don't really know why I was chosen for that type of work because, as I said, I wanted to become a psychic artist, but we all trusted the spirits completely. They must have had their reasons. We learned how to meditate and how to breathe and how to achieve total relaxation and visualisation. I learned how to meditate at a high level, which takes quite a few years. I heightened my vibrations to such a pitch that I could use my subconscious mind to enable myself to see spirits with my eyes shut during meditation! Fascinating!

When I first started to attend the circle, there were many happenings just to prove that the spirits were working with us. For instance, we had a plant in the middle of the room and we were told to concentrate on it. So we all sat round in a circle and

The Circle

watched intently and, to our amazement, the leaves started to move. It was as though they were being pulled down by some force and Phyllis, who was on the other side of the table, said, 'Oh, I didn't see that!' So the spirits moved the leaves on the other side as well, just so that she could see. We also saw water in a tumbler turn to wine and many other occurrences and we were all very excited. But, of course, once we progressed in meditation and listened to the words of wisdom from our guides we didn't need any more proof. I feel that knowledge and meditation are the keynotes to success in development.

It would be no use only attending a circle for, say, two years. No! Your guides will tell you when you are ready to work for spirit. Your guides can get quite frustrated, you know, particularly with people who do not listen to words of wisdom and haven't the patience to wait. That is why we have mediocre mediums instead of the elite. In the circle we also learned how to heal and used to give each other healing for practice. We were not allowed to heal outsiders until we had passed our apprenticeships or instructions. Once the guides knew that they could communicate through the healer and have complete control, we were ready. I am afraid that it is very easy for one's ego to get in the way and make the healer feel important. If this happens the guides will not work and will withdraw. To anyone who says to me 'Thank you very much', my response is, 'Thank my guides, for they are the healers.' We are but instruments.

All the time we are meditating as a circle and even at home, they are working on my eyes. They have done this for some time now, enabling me to see clearly with my eyes shut. It is like seeing in Technicolor, using the third eye. It really is fascinating and worth all the tedious waiting. This is why patience is so important.

I now return to the subject of healing. I am a magnetic healer. One day I found my hand shaking slightly. I questioned this in the circle and the guides told me through George, our medium in charge, that it was magnetic healing and that I would work in this way. I have done so ever since and it has been very effective. I do not heal now, however, unless someone requests it. There are certain rules from Brussels that I cannot follow, as I am in a

21

trance-like state when I am working by in order to follow the instructions given to me by my guide. I am guided by almighty God, his messengers or guides and no one else.

I remained in the circle for twenty years as we had all become great friends. While I was still there, the guides taught me how to go into light trances. A light trance is when spirits have control but you are still awake. As already mentioned, they built a spirit voice box in my throat to alter my voice for when they spoke through me and this took many years to achieve. I became accustomed to it as time went by, particularly once Red Wing, my Doctor Andrews and Wai Lai the Chinese Mandarin all spoke through me. The sitters used to look forward to the time when my guides came and conversed with them. Sometimes George, our medium and tutor, was used in this manner as well and we would have two trance mediums talking to each other. It was fascinating to have two guides in conversation.

Then a Japanese guide became very important to me. Her name was Su Shan Long and she informed me that she would help me with my psychic art. I was thrilled to have Su Shan Long to help me. She was quite pretty and I have her portrait now. While on the earth plane, Su Shan Long didn't have the chance to draw or paint although she was quite gifted – she had to support her brothers and sisters – but now she is happy to be able to help me. I painted a very big picture of an Indian encampment with Red Wing doing his rain dance. I also painted my other guides and those belonging to people in the circle, including Blue River, Sitting Bull, Silver Leaf and many others. I had confirmation from our guides that my paintings were accurate representations of them and this increased my confidence.

I can't stress enough the importance of meditation – it is how I reached such a high level. Nor can one rush these abilities; it takes many years to perfect your skills. However, not everyone has to wait as long as I did; it is possible to be ready after about five years, but you would have to take advice from your guides. I didn't have any difficulty staying all that time because I found it

The Circle

so enjoyable. There was something different every week.

I feel that meditation is very beneficial, even if one isn't striving for development, as it calms one right down. When I practise it, I feel so relaxed and in perfect harmony and forget all about everyday worries and problems. It is much better than taking tablets and pills to relax you. It is similar to yoga in that it controls the mind, encourages positive thinking and avoids negativity. Negativity halts your progress: it brings bad vibrations. Remember it is not good to think badly about anyone, because this creates negativity and that will rebound back on you twofold.

I must now tell you an interesting story about George, the medium who ran our circle, and how he became interested in starting it up. He had previously been a member of a circle run by Molly and John; they were mediums and very gifted rescue workers. They used to visit George and Martha on a Sunday and go for country drives in the car around Surrey and Sussex.

'Where shall we go?' George asked one day.

'Oh, let's just get lost!' said Molly.

So they found themselves going down a winding path, a very pretty country place. They stopped and wandered around; it was so enchanting, like a picture book.

Molly suddenly stopped and exclaimed, 'Oh look at that!'

There was a quaint old church. They all got rather excited and agreed to go in. The door was open but there was no one about so they all tiptoed in. Molly could see spirits but at that stage George could not; but he could feel and he had such a weight on his shoulders it made him quite nervous.

'I think I have someone with me,' he said.

'Don't worry,' said Molly, 'we will clear you when we get home.' John and Molly were rescue workers and took unwanted spirits away from people. They were very skilled at this, so when they arrived home, John and Molly held George's hands and, speaking quite softly, asked the spirits who they were and told them to 'Look to the Light and you will find your way'. The pressure went from George's head and he was cleared. Molly, being a strong medium, could see the lost spirit quite plainly. He was the spirit of an old man who had worked for the church giving out hymnbooks for hundreds of years. He was quite happy for that was all he understood. Ordinary folk would not be able to see him unless they were clairvoyants. Later that evening, a voice spoke through Molly, thanking them for rescuing him and Molly said, 'We were meant to meet you; it was ordained.' Amazing, isn't it, how spirits work! The old man saw the light and was helped into the spirit world where he could flourish and advance. This incident really inspired George to form his own circle to teach others and to help them develop and that is how he started.

I feel I have been spiritually guided to write this book. I feel it will enlighten many and open people's minds and make them more aware of spirits.

The world of today, I am afraid to say, is very aggressive and greedy. There are wars causing destruction of man in many countries. One cannot live in harmony. There will always be good and bad people on this earth plane but we are trying to give knowledge and understanding to those who will listen!

Although the universe in general is in a sorry state we also have many truly spiritual people around who are kind and considerate, loathe violence and are trying to help mankind in every way. This gives us the balance between good and evil.

You know, if you smile and are happy you send out good vibrations and people pick up on that and smile back. It makes them happy too. Did you know that the spiritual realms are sending old souls back to the earth plane to teach wisdom, compassion and understanding?

There is so much beauty here if only one can realise and think about it. It is a great shame that the majority of folk are too busy and occupied with jobs and mundane tasks. Of course, it is essential to work and earn a living but it would be nice to balance the two. Have you ever thought of the perfection of flowers? Really look at them: there are no flaws. Many people do not know or appreciate what they have: the true beauty of this planet; the wonders of these exotic birds with all their colourful plumage; the wonders of the mountains and the brilliant colours of the sunset – all breathtakingly beautiful. There are so many beautiful and

The Circle

wonderful sights to be seen and absorbed. Think of the wonderful vibrations that they are giving off! It is a great tonic to mankind.

How often have you heard the saying, 'You need a good holiday'? Yes, to unwind, recuperate, relax and find time to appreciate the wonders of nature; to be in complete harmony. That is a great tonic in itself! I have been in quite a few countries: Tunisia, Turkey, Spain and Morocco – only then do you understand real poverty. But amazingly the children are quite happy, always smiling and full of contentment. As long as they are fed and not hungry, they are happy. I often think about them. Western children of today do not realise how lucky they are to be born in England or other countries where there is plenty of food, clothes and all comforts. Yet they are not as happy as the Tunisians or the Turkish children who live in poverty. Strange, isn't it? I feel that sometimes one has too much but what can one do, when all the other children in the classroom get the same? You cannot isolate them – they would be very embarrassed.

I have two dogs now, cocker spaniels – one a blue roan and the other ginger and white. They are sisters and very close, both about seven and a half years old and thoroughly spoilt. They like a lot of loving and petting. They are so gentle and very affectionate – they just want to be made a fuss of. They are psychic and know when my guides are around. They go very quiet and stare, not knowing what to make of them; but they are used to them now. They are very good when I am drawing psychic guides or writing. They lie by my feet and sleep.

Since I started writing this book I have had another guide with me – Elizabeth Barrett Browning, famous for her poetry. Elizabeth was on the earth plane many years ago. She belonged to the Barretts of Wimpole Street in London and was renowned as one of the top poetesses of the time. I was of course quite excited about this. It would have been beyond my wildest dreams to be able to write in such an exquisite manner. As Elizabeth is a new guide with me, it will take a little while to adjust, but I am sure we will write many books in the future. I feel honoured and humbled to the spirits for giving me yet another guide. I am already helped and inspired with my psychic drawings and paintings and now I

How I Became a Psychic Artist

am being helped with my writing too! I am indeed very fortunate. My guides are not with me all the time, however; only when I start to work. The rest of the time, I just get on with my daily chores or go shopping just like everyone else.

It is nearly Christmas now and very cold outside. I shall be very busy shopping for presents and wrapping them up. I have a grown-up family – Michael, Pat, Jackie and Jill, eight grandchildren and five great-grandchildren – so I will be quite busy in this festive season – and this is on top of any clients I might have.

I do hope I have enlightened you with my reasons for becoming a psychic artist and I am truly grateful for the gifts that have been bestowed upon me. There is always a purpose and reason for being on the earth plane; it is a learning planet. Sometimes when you are down and depressed, try to remember there is always someone in spirit who is well aware of your plight: you are never alone. If we do not learn anything our lives will be negative and empty. I am not talking about academic learning; I mean learning about love and compassion, helping others, being kind, giving instead of taking. Some of the selfish and cruel people could reincarnate many times until they learn.

The world is in rather a mess – man-made – and the spirit world is not happy. Although man has free will he is foolish, for with his behaviour he could ultimately destroy the world. Now I am getting rather gloomy. But it is not all doom and gloom; we do have some wonderful people on this planet, caring folk who are doing their best to help and encourage others. We do not expect 'Holy Joes': we expect people to be kind and considerate to each other and kind to all animals. Of course we make mistakes, I often think, *If only I had done so and so*. But that is life. We learn from these mistakes.

I always feel so happy and grateful when I get such appreciative and wonderful letters back! It makes everything worthwhile. Indeed it makes me so humble to think that I was chosen for such a wonderful gift as psychic art and I am well aware that my wonderful guides help me. I still do the psychic drawings when requested, but I never advertise. I am now concentrating on writing my memoirs and trying to enlighten people of how and why I became a psychic artist. I have always looked much younger than my years and have never felt my age, although I have to admit I am quite old now.

The Circle

Perhaps it is because I am always so active.

Psychics are all very ordinary people, not weird or strange, just normal everyday folk. After our meetings we used to go down to the pub and enjoy ourselves. We would also go to a club and have social evenings. Sadly, after twenty years of activity, as most of the sitters had moved on, we decided to close the circle.

After I left the circle I used to go to psychic fairs as a psychic artist. A friend used to take me in her car and we would travel all over England. Once I was even invited to Tel-Aviv in Israel but had to decline the offer. I did this for about four years until I had an unfortunate accident, hitting my head which caused a heart attack and a stroke. I was taken to hospital. According to my daughter, Jackie, one side of my face dropped, as it does with a stroke, but it righted itself within a few days. Things were a bit blurred at the time but despite my injuries I remember feeling so peaceful and content. It was out of this world. I was just seventy then and I am sure I was being looked after. I am convinced that a miracle of healing happened to me that night. I was left only with angina which I have medication for. Unfortunately I cannot attend any more psychic fairs, but do work from home on request.

I remember a man – Roy was his name – who came to me for a reading and a drawing. He was very fed up and sad and he did not seem to have any aim in life. He was amazed at the sketch I did for him. Since I was talking to him and apparently not concentrating on the sketch he expected it to be a mere scribble. He remarked on how wonderful the detail was. As he left I said that I thought he could become a healer and again he was amazed. Roy later phoned me to tell me that on his way home he had met a lady who had taken him to a spiritual church in Graves End. He was in a bit of a daze but had gone with her and was now a healer in the making.

Roy was not allowed to heal patients for two years, he just healed other trainees, but after he had passed his apprenticeship he became a very strong healer. Roy is so devout and keen and is a very nice and caring man, spiritual through and through. He is now a different person from the Roy I originally met. He told me that I changed his life.

Quite a number of people have had their spiritual guides drawn; I send them by post now as I only need a photograph of the person to concentrate on. My guides do not need this, but I do. So you see, Roy has brought me quite a lot of work and still comes to see me from time to time.

I have such lovely letters from the people that I have drawn guides for; it makes me feel so happy and humble for having such a wonderful gift. Recently, I have been very busy drawing the spiritual guides of a lovely family from Hampshire. I also have Heather and Joan, former sitters in our circle. As they progress, they want their additional guides drawn for them. They live in Norfolk now but we keep in touch. I also do work for Sue, a very good medium who runs a circle in Suffolk. It is a great pity I am so far away from them all as we are such good friends.

In the circle to which I belonged there were many spiritual guides between us and they were all a source of learning and teaching. I have entered some of them in this book, but it would be impossible to say how many guides I have drawn; there are undoubtedly hundreds of them. I have sent many more by post, working from home following my illness. I like to work in complete solitude while drawing and painting to be in complete unison with my guides. When I draw the spiritual guides I feel so calm and serene and I seem to lose myself, forgetting all my troubles and worries, which is very good! I do feel quite honoured to do this work and feel I can bring joy and comfort to many people. If I have brought some happiness, I will feel that I have achieved my ambition in life. As well as giving me great satisfaction, my work has brought me many great friends, and I feel that I have helped them in some way. To enhance people's lives makes me feel contented and I have learned an awful lot. I hope you also have the enlightenment and comfort that I strive to give you.

It is very important to be positive most of the time. I say most of the time because it is virtually impossible to be positive all of the time. If you can be seventy per cent positive and only thirty per cent negative that will be satisfactory. Remember, the mind is stronger than the physical.

A Selection of Spiritual Guides

---

* Note: the guides are in colour originally.

The Venerable Bede

THIS spirit guide is an extremely high soul. He came from time to time to our circle to give advice and for inspection. He is higher than our other guides and visited other circles also. This is why he came only occasionally, but we always knew when he had arrived at our circle. We would whisper, 'The Venerable Bede is here!' because the room would go icy cold (even on a hot day!) and we would feel a distinct chill in our bones.

The Venerable Bede was a wonderful, gentle soul. He fulfilled the Holy Scripture either through the work of the Venerable Fathers, or in conformity with their meaning.

Doctor Andrews

WHAT a distinguished man he was! He was so kind and immaculate in every way. When he spoke through me, being highly educated and advanced, he would use very long words that I would normally have difficulty in pronouncing, let alone know the meaning of. Strangely enough, I had no difficulty while I was being used!

Although I do not continue with this type of work now, he will be with me until I pass over. This is unusual as working guides normally wish to continue their work as mentor and go to another person who is learning.

Sister Anne (A Nun)

SISTER Anne is so beautiful, with such wisdom in her eyes; the eyes are the mirror of the soul! She has been with me all my life though I did not really know this until I joined the circle. I had always sensed someone was there but had not known who. Sister Anne helps me to keep calm in extreme situations, protects me and guides me in the right direction. What a lovely kind and gentle spirit guide she is!

Su Shan Long

WHAT can I say! Where would I be without this beautiful and wonderful spirit guide who helps me so much? I only have to call upon her and she is at my side, guiding and influencing me. She loved drawing and painting, but unfortunately it was not possible while she was on the earth plane. Tragically orphaned, she worked as a geisha girl to support her younger brothers and sisters. Now she is happy to help me, for when I draw I forget everything else. I have such deep concentration – we do work well together! I am honoured to have her with me.

Wai Lai
(Chinaman from the Ming Dynasty)

*H*E is so fascinating, with such wisdom. The others in the circle were in awe and wonder at his wonderful conversation. He spoke in a typical Chinese manner and he had a sense of humour and used to make us laugh. But he was also so very polite – a lovely man! Wai Lai was a scribe for the emperor for many years and a devoted servant who was seen but not heard.

Elizabeth Barrett Browning

I HAVE recently acquired a new spirit guide called Elizabeth Barrett Browning to help me with my book. Elizabeth was a very famous poetess while on the earth plane, famed for her epic poetry. She resided with her family, the Barretts of Wimpole Street who, as you know, became quite famous. Elizabeth is a new guide and it will take a little while to become completely in harmony with her vibrations. I feel honoured to have her; she is such a learned and devout soul. I am sure we shall harmonise perfectly together!

Sister Isobel Bayliss

*A*LTHOUGH her first name was Isobel we always referred to her as 'Sister Bayliss'. She was a very compassionate and sympathetic spirit guide who helped Heather, giving her much comfort and confidence. She was with her to enhance her abilities for healing and Heather did indeed become a very devout and powerful healer with much sympathy and sensitivity. Knowing one is in such capable hands gives one an enormous amount of confidence.

Megan (Romany Gypsy)

A ROMANY gypsy, Megan is also Heather's guide and helps her with her skills as a medium, expanding her mind to be able to link with universal minds. She is also there for her protection. Megan would also inform Heather of the right kinds of herbs to keep her well and strong. The Romany are outdoor folk and very close to nature; they understand and respect all plant life as well as animals. They know that everything that is put on this earth plane has a purpose – plants, trees and every living creature.

Doctor Adams

*D*OCTOR Adams came to strengthen the power of George, our medium. He and the other spirits were taking George very deep into meditation, bringing him to a higher level of consciousness. Doctor Adams came with other groups of doctors to give strength and protection, for although George ran the circle he was still learning – one never stops learning!

Doctor Basehart

*D*OCTOR Basehart was the main guide in our circle. He spoke through George with such wisdom and culture and it was a pleasure to listen to him and acquire such knowledge. He was a Frenchman and spoke in broken English. It was fascinating to hear George in trance as he was a cockney himself.

Tia-le-Sonn

LATER on, I had clients writing to me asking for portraits of their guides. I was then working from home. One, a Tibetan monk named Tia-le-Sonn, was a very high guide. He used to go very high into the mountains where it was peaceful and tranquil, and would sit with crossed legs, meditating for days. Folk used to trek up the mountains hoping to get messages and to be blessed. They would wait quietly and patiently until the meditation was finished, then he would smile and bless them one by one. He was such a humble and devoted man and yet he also had radiance about him.

Rising Moon

*A*NOTHER client had a very powerful Native American guide, Rising Moon. Do you know how the Native Americans named their sons and daughters? The father took the baby from the mother as soon as it was born, took it outside and would name the baby after the first thing he saw, hence Rising Moon.

Pocahontas

*A*NOTHER client had Pocahontas as a guide. She was a beautiful Native American lady and quite well known. There is a memorial to her in Gravesend, England, where she was buried.

Red Wing (Cherokee)

RED Wing was the very first guide to speak through me. He was very powerful and forceful. Normally, in circles, the guide is chosen for their power and strength but must have a rapport and complete harmony with the sitter. When he was there I would feel so strong – he seemed to pull me upright! I felt very much like the Cherokee Red Wing, I felt his power.

Acquiring him as a guide was a gradual process. After many months he startled everyone by booming in his deep voice, 'Red Wing'. That is all he said to begin with but as the weeks went on he said more and more until we had whole conversations – it was fascinating!

Red Wing Camp

WHILE in the circle, I was commissioned to paint Red Wing and his life. He was a chief and was performing the rain dance around a camp fire, scattering the bones. All the guides of the circle were there – White Eagle, Blue River and Running Water. Children were on the right, and many squaws, their men and their children. Also, many used to come down from neighbouring tepees to see the rain dance; indeed they came from miles around. Messages travelled fast with their smoke signals and drums.

Lightning Source UK Ltd.
Milton Keynes UK
UKOW05f1803261113

221896UK00001B/21/A